𝒜 𝒶
𝒜𝑙𝑦𝑠𝒶
𝒶𝑙𝑙𝑖𝑔𝒶𝑡𝑜𝓇

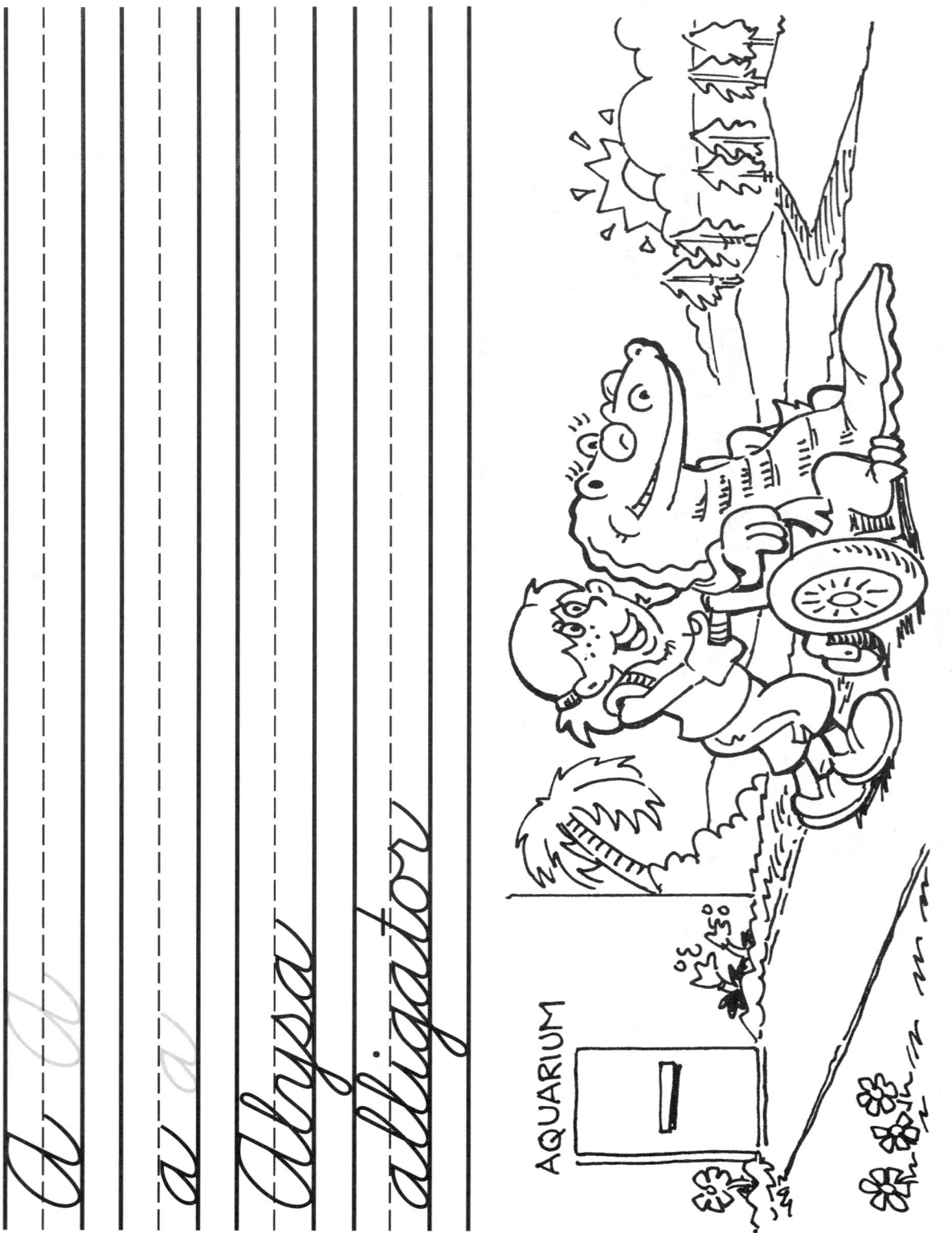

Alysa adopted an aging alligator from the aquarium.

𝐵 𝐵

𝑏 𝑏

Barbra

blueberry

Barbra and Bill baked blueberry biscuits for busy beetles.

C c

Colin

cosmic

Colin cleverly captured a crazy, cosmic creature.

D

d

Delaney

delivered

Delaney delivered delicious doughnuts to Dominick's Deli.

E E
l l
Ernie
escaped

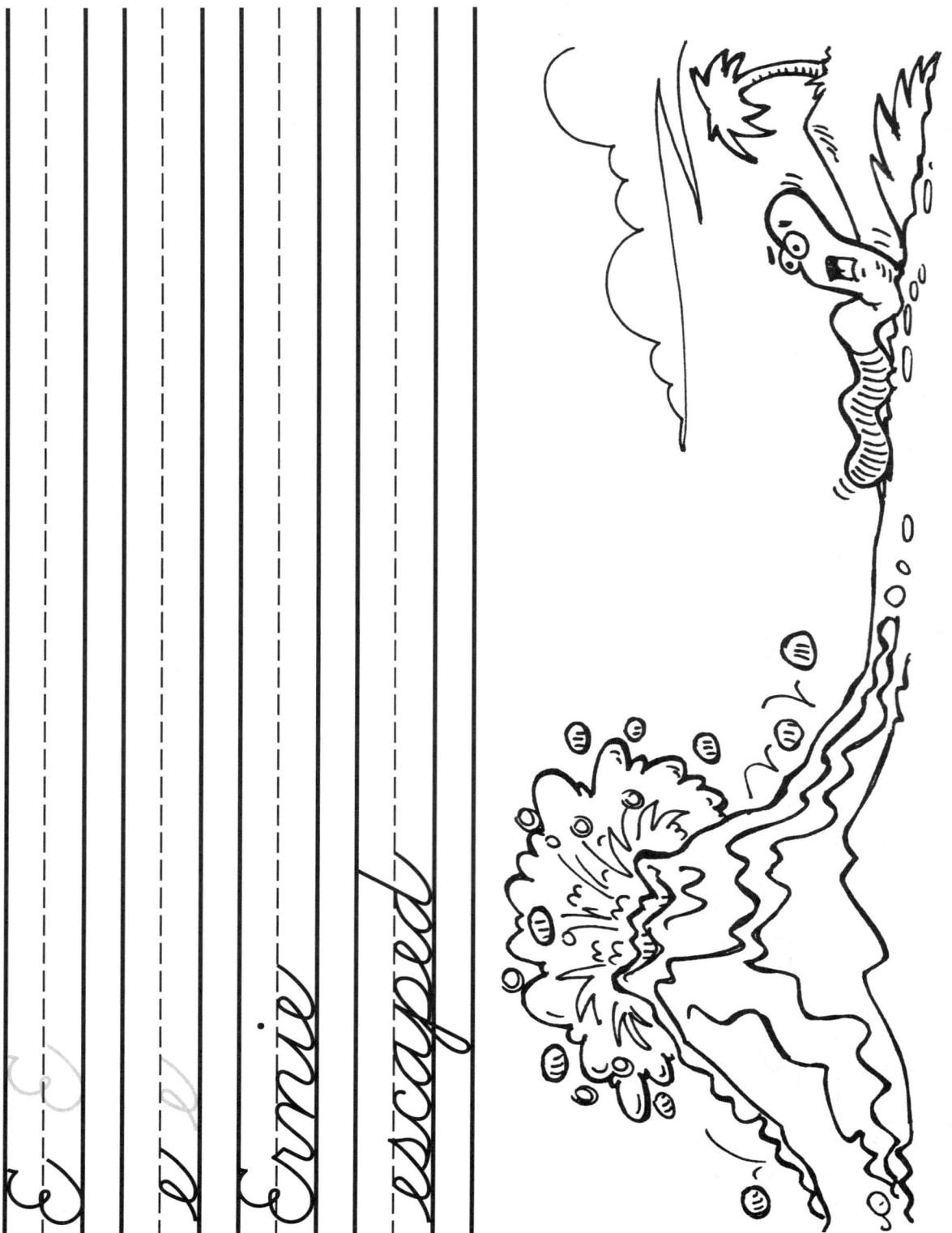

Ernie Earthworm
escaped the volcano's
eruption.

F f Fifi fireworks

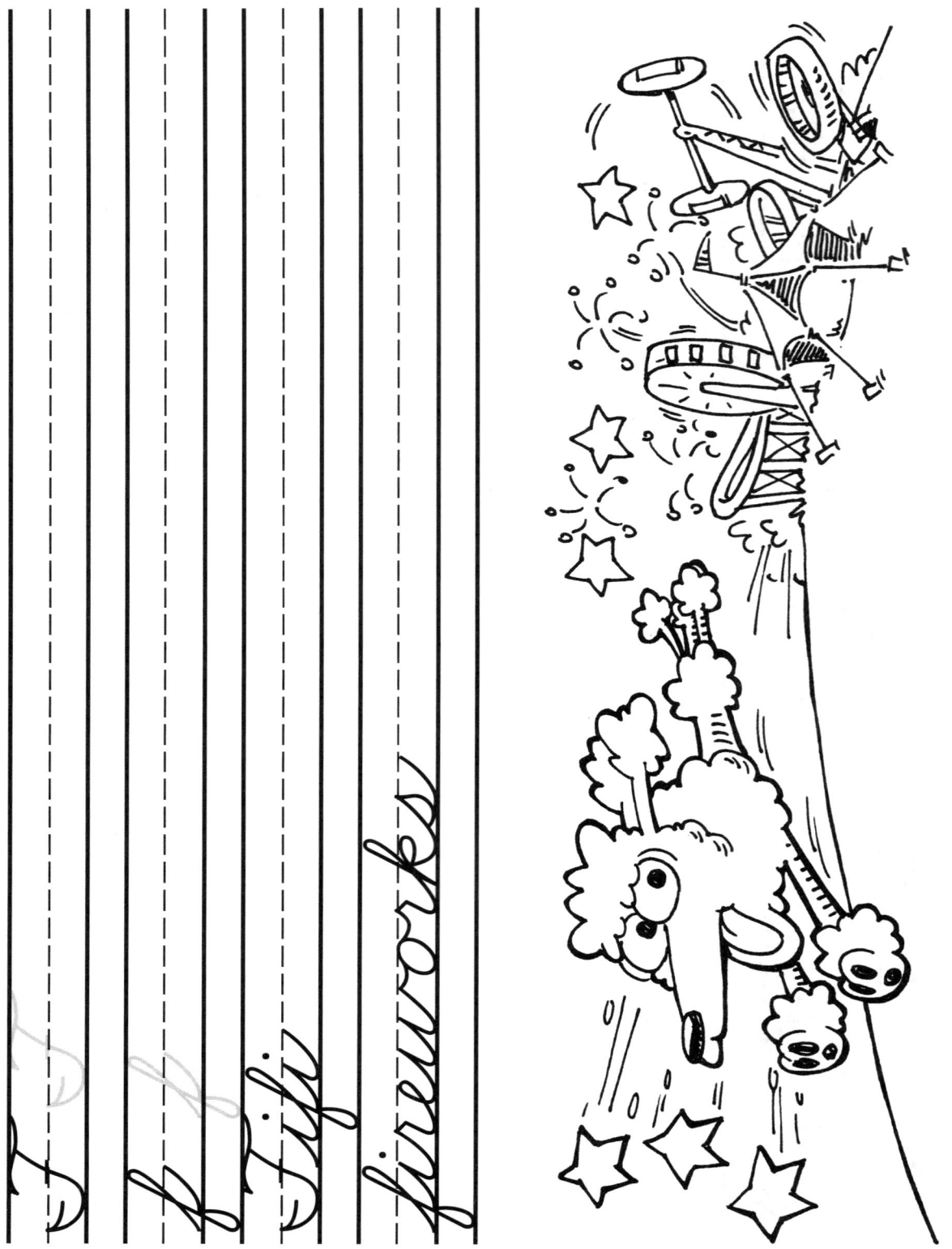

Fifi fled from the
flaming fireworks at
the fair.

G g Gregory grazing

Gregory gaped at the gentle giraffe grazing in the garden.

H h Hannah hippo

Hannah happily hugged the huge hippo on the hill.

Isabel invited

Isabel invited
interesting iguanas inn
for ice cream.

Jamal

jelly beans

Jamal juggled jelly

beans on his journey

into the jungle.

K
k
Kelly
kicking

Kelly found her
kangaroo kicking
ketchup in the kitchen.

ℒ ℓ

ℓ

Louis

leapfrog

Luis played leapfrog
in the library with
Leonard and Larry.

M M

m m

Michael

museum

Michael and Mark
made a muddy mess
in the museum.

n N

n n

Natasha

nightingales

Natasha never makes
noise near a new nest
of nightingales.

𝒪 𝒪 Olivia ocean

Olivia often observed
otters and ospreys out
on the ocean.

P P

p p

Pedro

purple

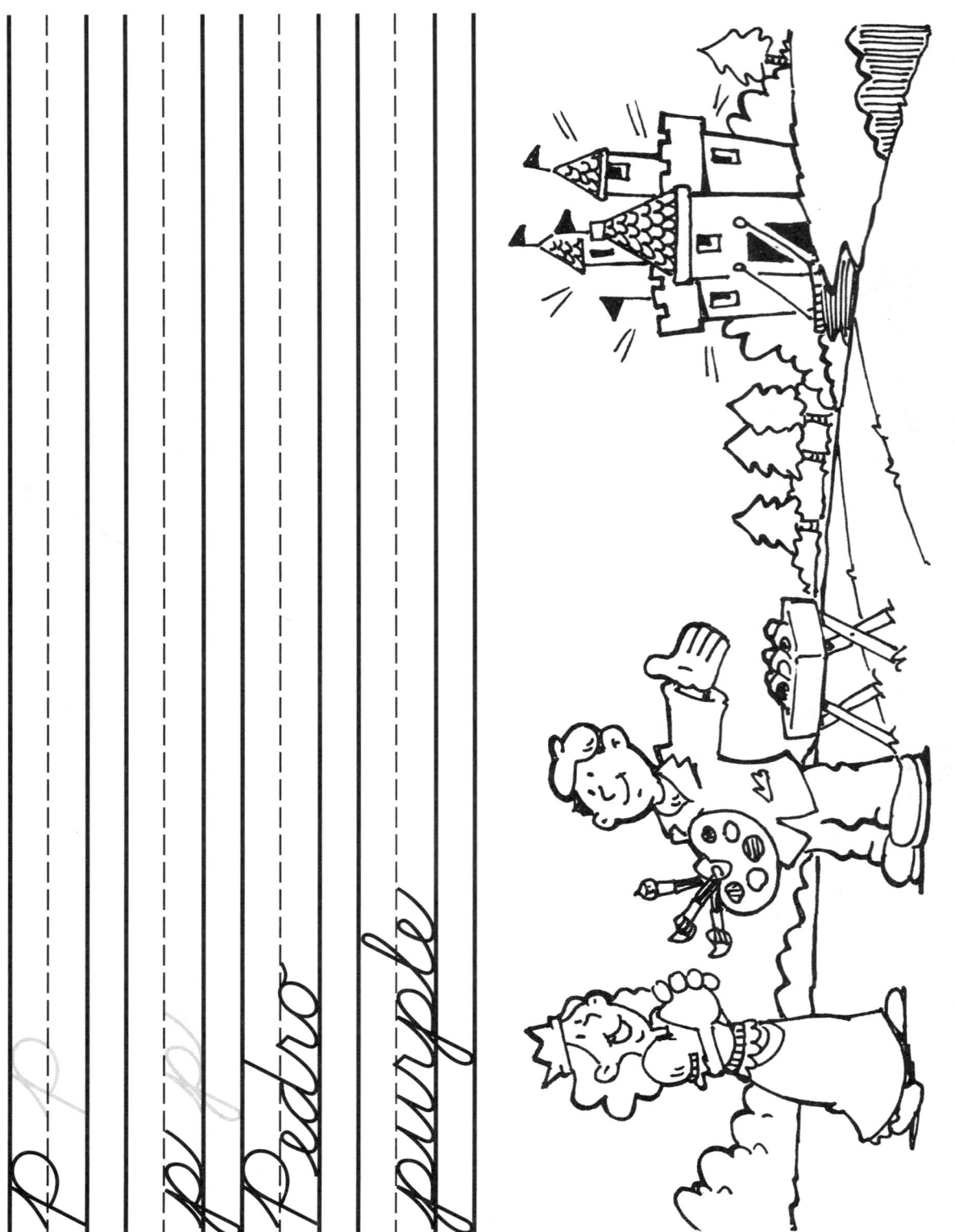

Pedro painted the palace purple and pink for the princess.

Q Q Quentin
quarter

Quentin quickly gave
the queen a quarter for
the quail.

R R
r r
Roberta
runner

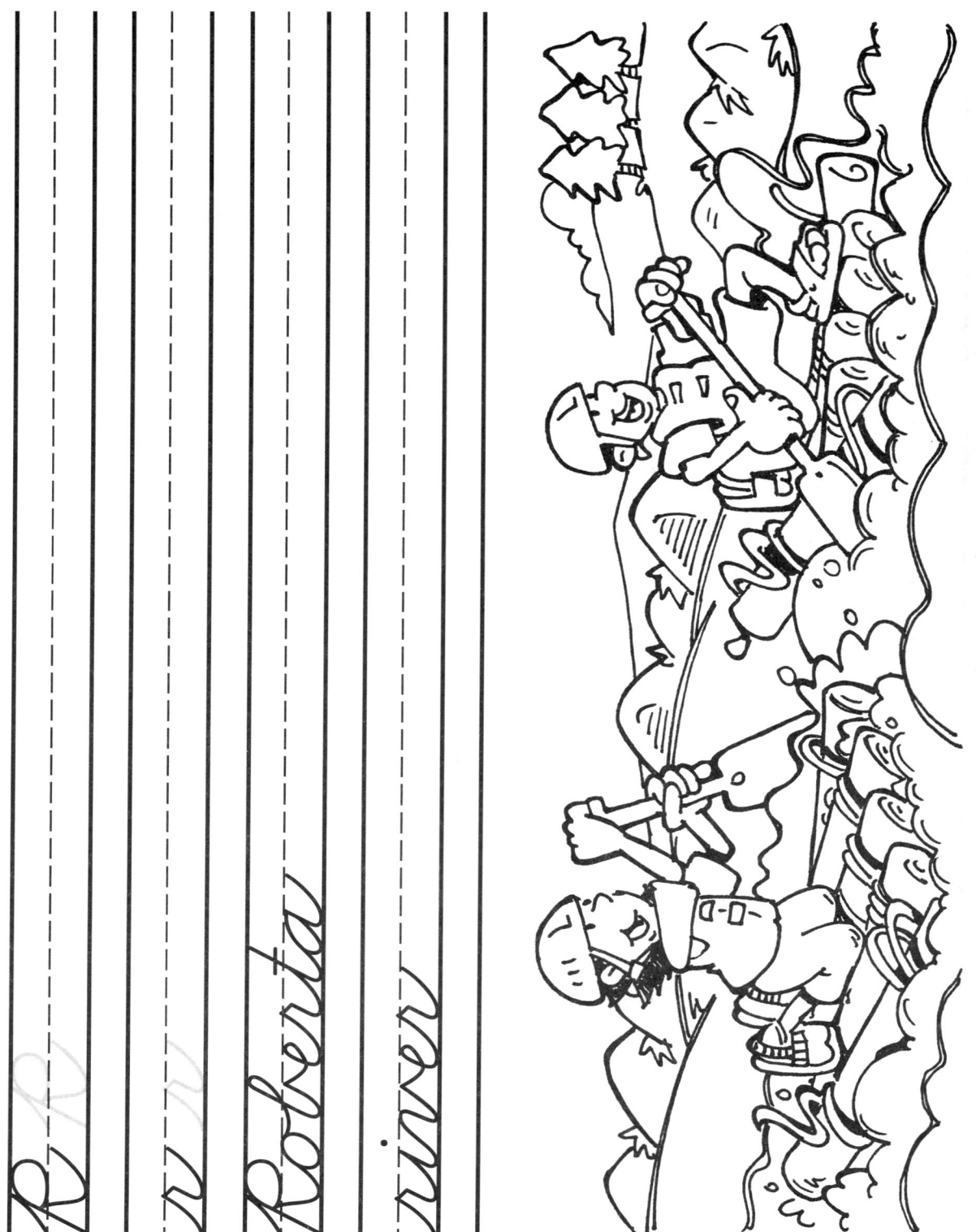

Roberta and Ronny raced rickety rafts on the river rapids.

S

Seth

strawberry

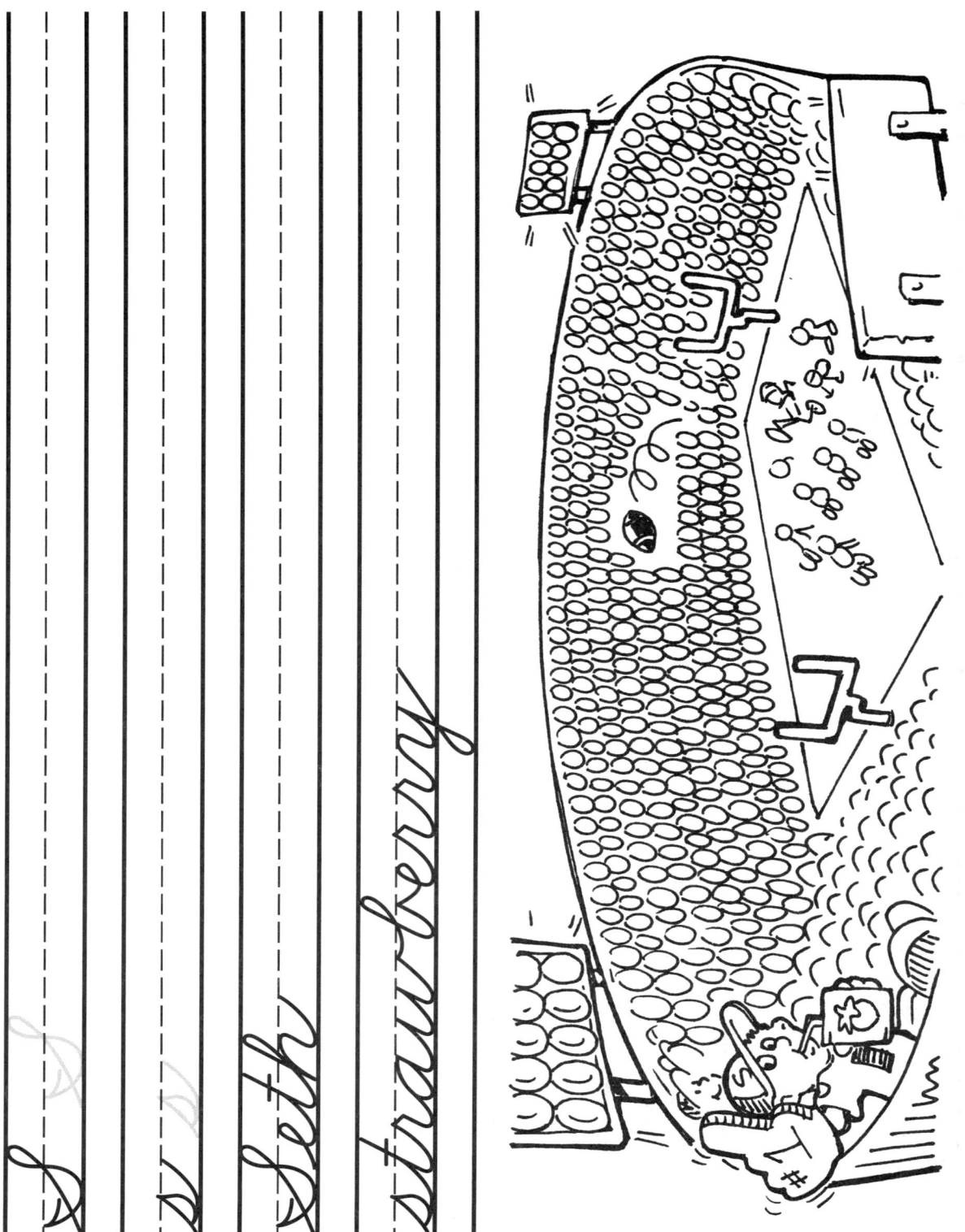

Seth sipped strawberry straws through a straw
soda through a straw
at the stadium.

T t Tamika tiger

Tamika taught tigers
to try tumbling tricks.

U u

Ursula

unicorn

Ursula and Uma

uncovered an unusual

unicorn under the tree.

V v Vincent vacation.

Vincent and Virginia
visited a variety of
volcanoes while on
vacation.

W W

w w

William

whales

In warm weather,
William walked to the
water to watch the
whales.

X x

xavier

exhibit

Xavier was excited to
find a row of foxes at
the exhibit.

Yy Yy Yolanda yummy

Yolanda yearned for

yummy yogurt and a

yellow yo-yo.

Z z Zeke zoomed

Zeke zipped and zoomed
through the zebra
house at the zoo.

Trace and write the numbers and number words.

0   zero
1   one
2   two
3   three
4   four
5   five
6   six
7   seven
8   eight
9   nine
10   ten

Trace and write the days of the week.

Sunday

Monday

Tuesday

Wednesday

Thursday

Friday

Saturday

Trace and write the months of the year on the lines below.

January

February

March

April

May

June

July

Trace and write the months of the year on the lines below.

August

September

October

November

December

Finish the sentences.

In summer, I like to _____

In fall, I like to _____

In winter, I like to _____

Finish the sentences.

In spring, I like to

My favorite season is because

Write each sentence in cursive.

I like to write in cursive.

Rachel's banana is almost ripe.

Laura has a blue dress and red shoes.

Write each sentence in cursive.

We built a fort under the tree.

Oscar feeds the birds in his yard.

Where is Felix's bookbag?

Write each sentence in cursive.

Kyle's first plane trip was last year.

Karla hit the baseball over the fence.

Frederico ate lunch with the twins.

Write each sentence in cursive.

Tasha picked a flower for her mom.

Today is Sampson's birthday.

Margaret likes to walk her dog.

Write each sentence in cursive.

Sabena is waiting for the bus.

How much did Alex grow last year?

Jennifer likes mushroom pizza.